WILD ANIMALS

WOLVERINES

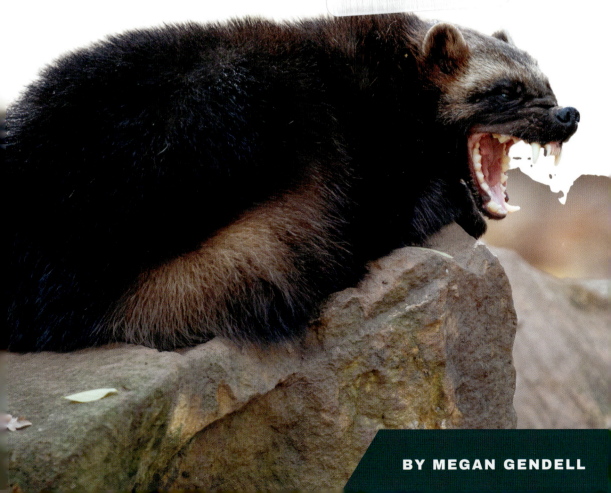

BY MEGAN GENDELL

WWW.APEXEDITIONS.COM

Copyright © 2023 by Apex Editions, Mendota Heights, MN 55120. All rights reserved. No part of this book may be reproduced or utilized in any form or by any means without written permission from the publisher.

Apex is distributed by North Star Editions:
sales@northstareditions.com | 888-417-0195

Produced for Apex by Red Line Editorial.

Photographs ©: Shutterstock Images, cover, 1, 4–5, 8, 10–11, 12–13, 14, 15, 16–17, 20–21, 22–23, 24, 29; Sylvain Cordier/Biosphoto/Alamy, 6–7; Stephen J. Krasemann/Science Source, 18–19; Ed Cesar/Science Source, 25; iStockPhoto, 26

Library of Congress Control Number: 2022910615

ISBN
978-1-63738-446-6 (hardcover)
978-1-63738-473-2 (paperback)
978-1-63738-524-1 (ebook pdf)
978-1-63738-500-5 (hosted ebook)

Printed in the United States of America
Mankato, MN
012023

NOTE TO PARENTS AND EDUCATORS

Apex books are designed to build literacy skills in striving readers. Exciting, high-interest content attracts and holds readers' attention. The text is carefully leveled to allow students to achieve success quickly. Additional features, such as bolded glossary words for difficult terms, help build comprehension.

TABLE OF CONTENTS

CHAPTER 1
FOOD FOR LATER 4

CHAPTER 2
BUILT FOR WINTER 10

CHAPTER 3
FINDING FOOD 16

CHAPTER 4
LIFE IN THE WILD 22

COMPREHENSION QUESTIONS • 28
GLOSSARY • 30
TO LEARN MORE • 31
ABOUT THE AUTHOR • 31
INDEX • 32

CHAPTER 1

FOOD FOR LATER

A wolverine has been running for miles. She stops and stands on her back legs. She sniffs the air to search for food.

A wolverine's sense of smell is very strong.

Her nose catches the scent of a dead deer. Another animal killed the deer, ate some, and left. The wolverine can eat the leftovers.

WHAT'S THAT SMELL?

A wolverine's body makes a stinky spray. The wolverine covers its food with this smell. That way, other animals won't take the food.

Wolverines can smell dead animals that are far away or buried in snow.

The wolverine tears off part of the dead deer. She hides it under a big rock. She will come back for it in spring. It will help feed her babies.

FAST FACT
Wolverines use their sharp claws to dig and bury food.

Wolverines have strong muscles. They can move rocks that are twice their own weight.

CHAPTER 2

BUILT FOR WINTER

Wolverines are small, furry **mammals**. They live in northern parts of Asia, Europe, and North America. They often live in mountain forests.

Many wolverines live in places with lots of trees and deep snow.

In winter, wolverine **habitats** are cold and snowy. Thick fur helps wolverines stay warm. And big paws help them run on top of deep snow.

In the past, people hunted wolverines for their warm fur.

FANCY FUR

A wolverine's fur is black or brown. A yellowish stripe often runs down the animal's side. Each wolverine has a unique color pattern. No two are the same.

Wolverines have short legs and long, fluffy tails. They have strong jaws. Their sharp teeth can tear into frozen meat.

A wolverine's teeth can bite through bone.

Male wolverines can weigh 24 to 40 pounds (11–18 kg).

FAST FACT

Sharp claws help wolverines climb hills and trees.

CHAPTER 3

FINDING FOOD

Wolverines hunt at night. They travel for miles in search of food. Sometimes they catch small animals.

Wolverines eat some plants. But they mostly eat meat.

Wolverines may also hunt large animals such as moose and deer. These animals move slowly in deep snow. Wolverines run faster. They can kill big animals that are hurt or weak.

Wolverines may travel 15 miles (24 km) each day to find food.

WOLF DANGER

Wolverines eat lots of different prey. But not many animals eat wolverines. Wolves are their main predators. Wolves kill young wolverines.

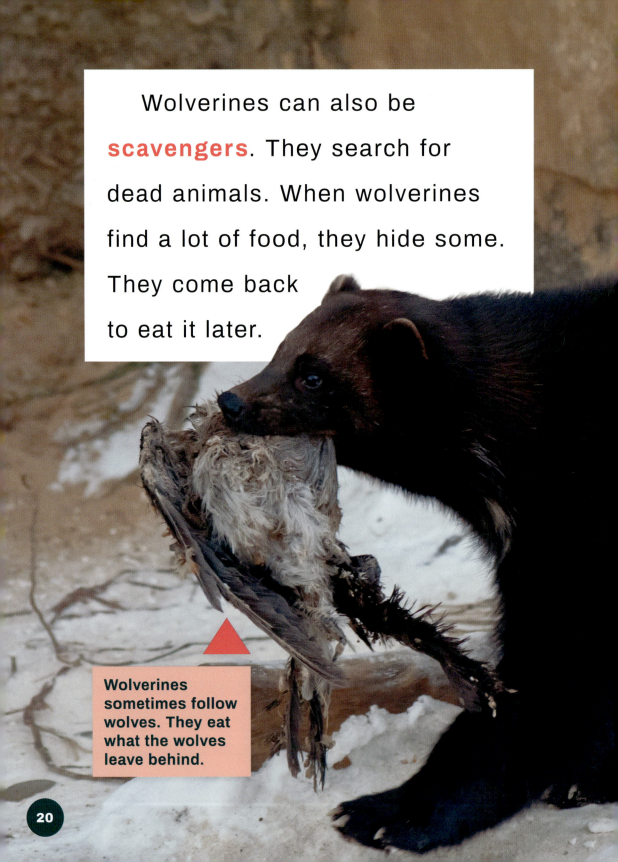

Wolverines can also be **scavengers**. They search for dead animals. When wolverines find a lot of food, they hide some. They come back to eat it later.

Wolverines sometimes follow wolves. They eat what the wolves leave behind.

FAST FACT

Foxes hide food to eat later. Wolverines follow foxes. They steal the hidden food.

CHAPTER 4

LIFE IN THE WILD

Most adult wolverines live alone. Males mark their **territory** with scents. They might fight other wolverines that come near.

Wolverines usually live 7 to 12 years in the wild.

Wolverines sleep in their dens during the day.

Wolverines come together to **mate**. Females give birth in late winter. They usually have one to three **kits**. The kits are born in dens under the snow.

24

FAST FACT

Wolverine kits are born with white fur. They blend in with the snow.

When wolverine kits are first born, they are tiny and can't see. Dens keep them safe and warm.

By the next winter, the kits are fully grown. They are ready to live on their own. But some live near their mothers for another year. Then they go have their own babies.

COME OUT AND PLAY
Wolverines are fierce hunters. They bite their prey's necks to kill the prey. But wolverines can be playful, too. In winter, they roll around in the snow.

Wolverines are smart and curious. They sometimes play together.

COMPREHENSION QUESTIONS

Write your answers on a separate piece of paper.

1. Write a few sentences describing the different kinds of food that wolverines eat.

2. Wolverines hunt at night. Would you rather stay up late or wake up early? Why?

3. In what season are baby wolverines born?
- **A.** spring
- **B.** summer
- **C.** winter

4. Why would wolverines hunt big animals that are hurt or weak?
- **A.** Those animals move slower, so they are easier to hunt.
- **B.** Those animals are old, so they taste better.
- **C.** Those animals are louder, so they are easier to find.

5. What does **unique** mean in this book?

Each wolverine has a unique color pattern. No two are the same.

    A. all exactly alike
    B. lighter than any other
    C. different from any other

6. What does **fierce** mean in this book?

Wolverines are fierce hunters. They bite their prey's necks to kill the prey.

    A. cute and fluffy
    B. scary and strong
    C. bad at fighting

Answer key on page 32.

GLOSSARY

habitats
The places where animals normally live.

kits
Newly born furry animals.

mammals
Animals that have hair and produce milk for their young.

mate
To form a pair and come together to have babies.

predators
Animals that hunt and eat other animals.

prey
Animals that are hunted and eaten by other animals.

scavengers
Animals that eat dead animals they did not kill.

territory
An area that an animal or group of animals lives in and defends.